Trumpet

Level 2–3

STRUMENTAL
LAY-ALONG

ONLINE
ACCESS
INCLUDED

- Professional Recordings
- Practice Software
- Piano Accompaniments

Top Broadway and MOVIE Songs

TRUMPET

REMEMBER US THIS WAY

SMALL FOOT

SHALLOW

BALBOA
THE BEST OF ROCKY

I'LL NEVER LOVE AGAIN
A STAR IS BORN

HAMILTON
AN AMERICAN MUSICAL

LITTLE SHOP OF HORRORS

MAMMA MIA!

OVER THE RAINBOW

IS THAT ALRIGHT?

TOP GUN

LA LA LAND

ISBN-10: 1-4706-4229-8 (Book & Online Audio/Software/PDF)
ISBN-13: 978-1-4706-4229-7 (Book & Online Audio/Software/PDF)

Arranged by Bill Galliford and Ethan Neuburg

Audio recordings produced by Dan Warner, Doug Emery, and Lee Levin

CONTENTS

TNT 2 System Requirements

Windows
10, 8, 7
QuickTime 7.6.7 or higher
1.8 GHz processor or faster
360 MB hard drive space
2 GB RAM minimum
Speakers or headphones
Internet access for updates

Macintosh
OS 10.4 and higher (Intel only)
QuickTime 7.6.7 or higher
470 MB hard drive space
2 GB RAM minimum
Speakers or headphones
Internet access for updates

OVER THE RAINBOW

(from *The Wizard of Oz*)

Lyric by
E.Y. HARBURG

Music by
HAROLD ARLEN

SHALLOW
(from *A Star Is Born*)

Words and Music by
LADY GAGA, MARK RONSON,
ANTHONY ROSSOMANDO and ANDREW WYATT

Moderate folk rock (♩ = 96)

Shallow - 2 - 1

ALWAYS REMEMBER US THIS WAY

(from *A Star Is Born*)

Words and Music by
LADY GAGA, NATALIE HEMBY,
HILLARY LINDSEY and LORI McKENNA

Moderately slow folk rock (♩ = 66)

Always Remember Us This Way - 2 - 1

DEMO **6** | PLAY-ALONG **7**

© 2018 WARNER-BARHAM MUSIC LLC (BMI), WARNER-OLIVE MUSIC LLC (ASCAP), SONY/ATV SONGS LLC (BMI), HOUSE OF GAGA PUBLISHING LLC (BMI),
SG SONGS (BMI), HAPPYGOWRUCKE (BMI), CREATIVE PULSE MUSIC (BMI), BIRB MUSIC (ASCAP) and MAPS AND RECORDS MUSIC (BMI)
All Rights for WARNER-BARHAM MUSIC LLC (BMI) Administered by SONGS OF UNIVERSAL, INC. (BMI)
All Rights on behalf of WARNER-OLIVE MUSIC LLC (ASCAP) Administered by UNIVERSAL MUSIC GROUP (ASCAP)
All Rights on behalf of HAPPYGOWRUCKE (BMI), CREATIVE PULSE MUSIC (BMI) and MAPS AND RECORDS MUSIC (BMI) Administered by THESE ARE PULSE SONGS (BMI)
All Rights on behalf of BIRB MUSIC (ASCAP) Administered by BMG RIGHTS MANAGEMENT (US) (ASCAP)
All Rights on behalf of SONY/ATV SONGS (BMI) and HOUSE OF GAGA PUBLISHING LLC (BMI)
Administered by SONY/ATV MUSIC PUBLISHING LLC, 424 Church Street, Suite 1200, Nashville, TN 37219
Exclusive Print Rights on behalf of WARNER-BARHAM MUSIC LLC (BMI) and WARNER-OLIVE MUSIC LLC (ASCAP) Administered by ALFRED MUSIC
All Rights Reserved

DEMO 8 | PLAY-ALONG 9

LOOK WHAT I FOUND

(from *A Star Is Born*)

Words and Music by
LADY GAGA, PAUL BLAIR,
NICK MONSON, LUKAS NELSON,
MARK NILAN JR. AND AARON RAITIERE

Moderate pop rock (♩ = 98)

Look What I Found - 2 - 1

I'LL NEVER LOVE AGAIN

(from *A Star Is Born*)

Words and Music by
LADY GAGA, NATALIE HEMBY,
HILLARY LINDSEY and AARON RAITIERE

I'll Never Love Again - 2 - 1

DEMO **12** | PLAY-ALONG **13**

ANOTHER DAY OF SUN
(from *La La Land*)

Music by JUSTIN HURWITZ
Lyrics by BENJ PASEK & JUSTIN PAUL

Another Day of Sun - 2 - 1

DEMO **14** | PLAY-ALONG **15**

CITY OF STARS
(from *La La Land*)

Music by JUSTIN HURWITZ
Lyrics by BENJ PASEK & JUSTIN PAUL

Moderately (♩ = 104) (♫ = ♪³♪)

City of Stars - 2 - 1

YOU'LL BE BACK

(from the Broadway musical *Hamilton*)

Words and Music by
LIN-MANUEL MIRANDA

You'll Be Back - 2 - 1

WONDERFUL LIFE

(from *Smallfoot*)

Words and Music by
WAYNE KIRKPATRICK
and KAREY KIRKPATRICK

World folk rock (♩ = 103)

Wonderful Life - 2 - 1

DANGER ZONE
(from *Top Gun*)

Words and Music by
GIORGIO MORODER and TOM WHITLOCK

Danger Zone - 2 - 1

DEMO **22** | PLAY-ALONG **23**

EYE OF THE TIGER
(from *Rocky III*)

Words and Music by
FRANKIE SULLIVAN III and JIM PETERIK

Moderate rock (♩ = 110)

MAMMA MIA!

Words and Music by
BENNY ANDERSSON, STIG ANDERSON
and BJORN ULVAEUS

Moderately bright (♩ = 136)

DEMO **26** | PLAY-ALONG **27**

SUDDENLY, SEYMOUR
(from *Little Shop of Horrors*)

Words by
HOWARD ASHMAN

Music by
ALAN MENKEN

Suddenly, Seymour - 2 - 1

PARTS OF A TRUMPET AND FINGERING CHART

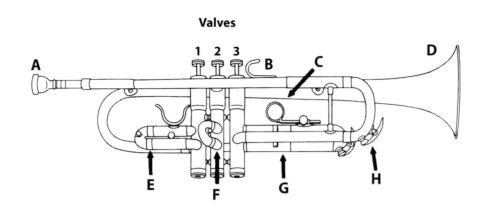

A – Mouthpiece

B – "Pinky" Ring

C – Finger Ring

D – Bell

E – First Valve Slide

F – Second Valve Slide

G – Third Valve Slide

H – Water Key

When two enharmonic notes are given together (F♯ and G♭ for example), they sound the same pitch and are played the same way.

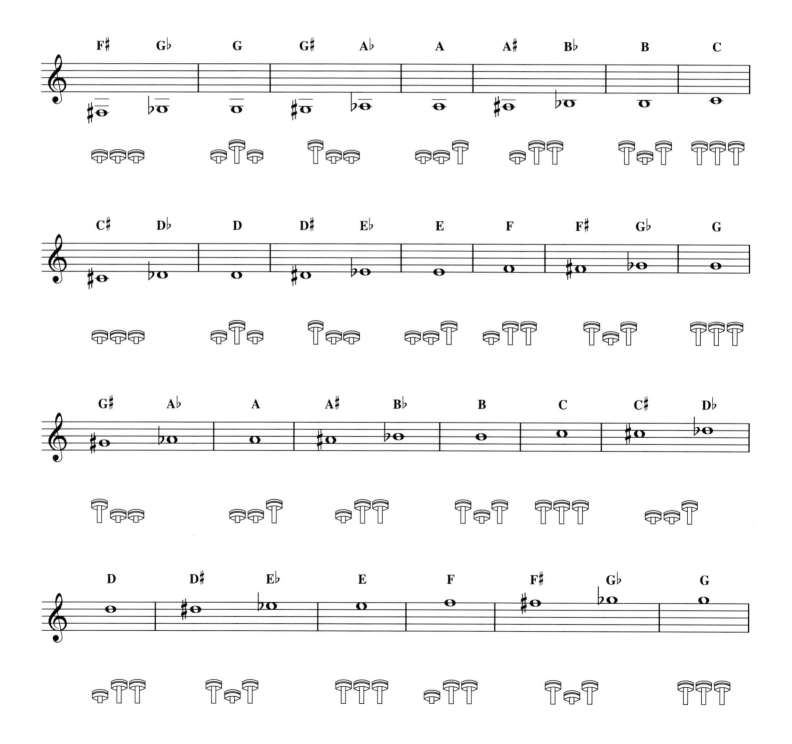

Make Your Playlist Your Practice List

Professional Recordings • TNT 2 Practice Software • Piano Accompaniments

Grade 1

Easy Classical Themes Instrumental Solos

Titles: Spring (Vivaldi) • Ode to Joy (Beethoven) • Largo (Dvořák) • Canon in D (Pachelbel) • Dance of the Sugar Plum Fairy (Tchaikovsky) • Trepak (Russian Dance) (Tchaikovsky) • Air on the G String (Bach) • Minuet in G Major (Petzold/Bach) • Für Elise (Beethoven) • Brahms' Lullaby (Brahms) • Rondeau (Masterpiece Theatre theme) (Mouret) • Andante (from the "Surprise" Symphony) (Haydn) • Morning Mood (Grieg) • Habanera (Bizet) • Can-Can (Offenbach).

Flute (00-47044)	Trumpet (00-47056)
Clarinet (00-47047)	Horn in F (00-47059)
Alto Sax (00-47050)	Trombone (00-47062)
Tenor Sax (00-47053)	

Easy Pop & Rock Hits Instrumental Solos

Titles: Best Day of My Life (American Authors) • Best Song Ever (One Direction) • Daylight (Maroon 5) • Firework (Katy Perry) • Girl on Fire (Alicia Keys) • Home (Philip Phillips) • I Need Your Love (Calvin Harris, featuring Ellie Goulding) • I See Fire (Ed Sheeran) • Just Give Me a Reason (Pink and Nate Ruess) • Just the Way You Are (Amazing) (Bruno Mars) • Roar (Katy Perry) • Stay the Night (Zedd, featuring Hayley Williams) • We Are Young (fun.).

Flute (00-42975)	Trumpet (00-42987)
Clarinet (00-42978)	Horn in F (00-42990)
Alto Sax (00-42981)	Trombone (00-42993)
Tenor Sax (00-42984)	

Grade 2–3

Pop & Country Instrumental Solos

Titles: Shape of You (Ed Sheeran) • Feel It Still (Portugal. The Man) • How Long (Charlie Puth) • There's Nothing Holdin' Me Back (Shawn Mendes) • Attention (Charlie Puth) • Say Something (Justin Timberlake, featuring Chris Stapleton) • Believer (Imagine Dragons) • Meant to Be (Bebe Rexha, featuring Florida Georgia Line) • One Foot (Walk the Moon) • Havana (Camila Cabello, featuring Young Thug) • The Champion (Carrie Underwood, featuring Ludacris) • Broken Halos (Chris Stapleton).

Flute (00-47327)	Trumpet (00-47339)
Clarinet (00-47330)	Horn in F (00-47342)
Alto Sax (00-47333)	Trombone (00-47345)
Tenor Sax (00-47336)	

Harry Potter™ Instrumental Solos

Titles: Double Trouble • Family Portrait • Farewell to Dobby • Fawkes the Phoenix • Fireworks • Harry in Winter • Harry's Wondrous World • Hedwig's Theme • Hogwarts' Hymn • Hogwarts' March • Leaving Hogwarts • Lily's Theme • Obliviate • Statues • A Window to the Past • Wizard Wheezes.

Flute (00-39211)	Trumpet (00-39223)
Clarinet (00-39214)	Horn in F (00-39226)
Alto Sax (00-39217)	Trombone (00-39229)
Tenor Sax (00-39220)	

Star Wars® Instrumental Solos (Movies I–VI)

Music by John Williams

Titles: Star Wars (Main Theme) • Qui-Gon's Funeral • Duel of the Fates • Anakin's Theme • The Meadow Picnic • Battle of the Heroes • Cantina Band • The Throne Room • The Imperial March • Princess Leia's Theme • and more.

Flute (00-32101)	Trumpet (00-32113)
Clarinet (00-32104)	Horn in F (00-32116)
Alto Sax (00-32107)	Trombone (00-32119)
Tenor Sax (00-32110)	

Hit Movie & TV Instrumental Solos

Titles: Amazons of Themyscira (Wonder Woman) • Another Day of Sun (La La Land) • Beauty and the Beast (Beauty and the Beast) • City of Stars (La La Land) • Everything Is Awesome (The LEGO® Batman Movie) • Ghostbusters (Ghostbusters) • Heathens (Suicide Squad) • Just Like Fire (Alice Through the Looking Glass) • Kowalski Rag (Fantastic Beasts and Where to Find Them) • A Man and His Beasts (Fantastic Beasts and Where to Find Them) • Mia & Sebastian's Theme (La La Land) • Newt Says Goodbye to Tina / Jacob's Bakery (Fantastic Beasts and Where to Find Them) • Runnin' Home to You (The Flash) • Westworld: Opening Theme (Westworld).

Flute (00-46753)	Trumpet (00-46765)
Clarinet (00-46756)	Horn in F (00-46768)
Alto Sax (00-46759)	Trombone (00-46771)
Tenor Sax (00-46762)	